HOW TO TALK
SO Men
WILL LISTEN

HOW TO TALK SO MEN WILL LISTEN. Copyright © 2021 by St. Martin's Press.
All rights reserved. Printed in the United States of America.
For information, address St. Martin's Publishing Group, 120 Broadway, New York, NY 10271.

www.castlepointbooks.com

The Castle Point Books trademark is owned by Castle Point Publishing, LLC.
Castle Point books are published and distributed by St. Martin's Publishing Group.

ISBN 978-1-250-27648-3 (trade paperback)

Our books may be purchased in bulk for promotional, educational, or business use.
Please contact your local bookseller or the Macmillan Corporate and Premium Sales Department
at 1-800-221-7945, extension 5442, or by email at MacmillanSpecialMarkets@macmillan.com.

First Edition: 2021

10 9 8 7 6 5 4 3 2 1

HOW TO TALK

A COLORING BOOK

SO MEN

WILL LISTEN

CAITLIN PETERSON
ILLUSTRATED BY JASON MILLET

CASTLE POINT BOOKS
NEW YORK

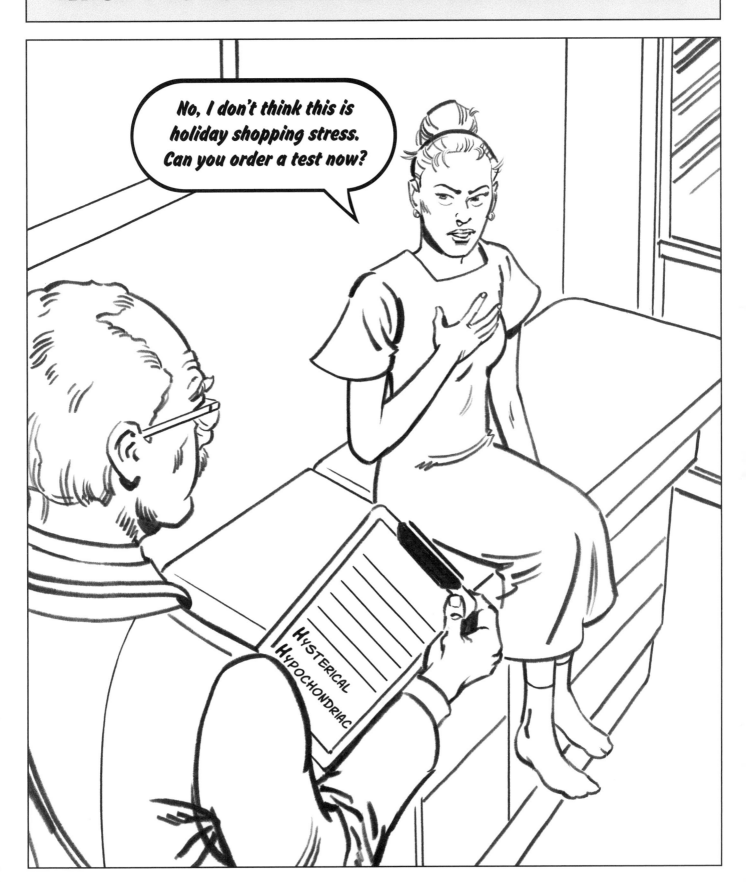

WHEN HE TALKS ABOUT HIMSELF TOO LONG:

WHEN CREDIBILITY ISN'T ALWAYS A GIVEN:

WHEN YOU'RE OFFERED A JOB WITH INSULTINGLY LOW PAY:

WHEN YOU GET TREATED LIKE A SECRETARY:

WHEN HE SAYS YOU'RE TOO BOSSY:

HOW TO DRESS FOR THE OFFICE:

HOW TO TALK SO MEN WILL LISTEN: